OF LOVE AND DESIRE

Also by Louis de Bernières

Louis de Bernières

OF LOVE AND DESIRE

ILLUSTRATED BY DONALD SAMMUT

Harvill *Secker*

LONDON

10 9 8 7 6 5 4 3 2 1

Harvill Secker, an imprint of Vintage,
20 Vauxhall Bridge Road,
London SW1V 2SA

Harvill Secker is part of the Penguin Random House
group of companies whose addresses can be found
at global.penguinrandomhouse.com

Copyright © Louis de Bernières 2016
Illustrations © Donald Sammut 2016

Louis de Bernières has asserted his right to be identified
as the author of this work in accordance with
the Copyright, Designs and Patents Act 1988

First published by Harvill Secker in 2016

www.vintage-books.co.uk

A CIP catalogue record for this book is available from the British Library

ISBN 9781846558849

Typeset in Dante MT by Palimpsest Book Production Ltd, Falkirk, Stirlingshire
Printed and bound in Germany by GGP Media GmbH, Pössneck

Penguin Random House is committed to a sustainable future
for our business, our readers and our planet. This book is made
from Forest Stewardship Council® certified paper

Dedicated to my Father, Piers

Car l'esprit ne sent rien que par l'ayde du corps.

RONSARD

CONTENTS

I LEANED DOWN FROM THE SADDLE

I leaned down from the saddle,
Took the cup from your hand
And drained away the wine.

You said that in the mountains
I'd find what I was after
If I was tired of life.

You said the high white clouds
Would freeze the darkness out
And wash my tarnished soul.

I leaned down from the saddle,
Returned the cup to your hand
And gave you three bronze coins.

You said that, should I pass that way,
You'd keep aside some wine
As rich, as fine as this.

FOR LAURA ANADYOMENE CYTHERAEA

It's you I envy, with your maiden eyes that gaze
On Greece for the first time; the casual flick
Of the lighthouse, the Cyprus trees like
Soldiers, the castle quiet with ghosts
On the high white crag awash
With flowers and bees, above
The gentle wrinkled sea where
The sky's half blind in mirrored light.
It's you I envy, newly drenched in
Vapour of the rock-sprung thyme,
You, of skyblue eyes, soft speech and
Vivid heart and sungold hair, as fresh
As Afrodite, also born of foam,
Who wrings her tresses on her
Shoulder, you and she as
Lovely as each other, and
As lovely as this land.

HAVING FAILED TO MAKE
HER ENJOY FISHING

If the
Sun sinks much more,
If my love becomes more bored
I will have to stop this fishing. And
What a shame. The river's calm, serene,
The painted flies are hatching by the reeds.
It's the best time, the holy time, when
The fish feed in the last light, and
Bubbles rise up from the mud,
And kingfishers perch on the
Tip of the rod, and the sun's
Like a flaming scarlet dish,
And oh what a shame,
My love is bored
Is yearning to leave,
And longs for home,
And caught the largest fish.

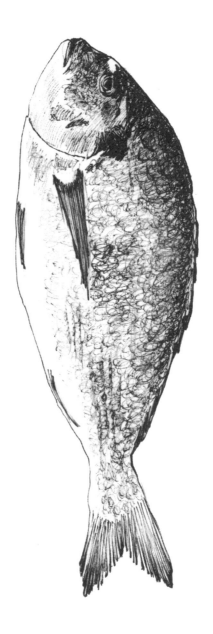

I TRAVELLED SOUTH

I travelled South past fen and town and field,
Past warehouse, village, wood and stream, across
The mud-brown Thames, that water-road, its bridge
Raised up by Titans, cargo ships moored up
Against the banks, vainglorious towers far off,
And swans asleep in autumn's waning sun.

I skirted round the foot of breasted hills that rose
At either flank where I grew tall,
And saw beloved landscapes, strangely fresh,
That then I hardly saw or loved at all.

And this was all to seek you out,
To pass a day with you and prove,
As I have never doubted once,
That forty years ago, when we were new,
How right I was to love you as I did.

ON THE LAST NIGHT WHEN LOVE WAS LORD

On the last night when Love was lord
And hosted us, invisible as we ate,
We left the table laughing,
Tipped back the final heels of wine,
Gave up the remnant of the feast,
As lovers have the right to do,
And took to bed, unheeding of
The candles, burning on, that wept
Their tortuous trails of wax
Till all their tears grew solid on the cloth.

Then I awoke at dawn and, at the bedroom
Window, watched Love leave, his cloak wrapped
Tight around him, striding out across the field
As if in flight from some disgrace,
As if in flight from flood or war.
And down amid the remnant of the feast,
Amongst the clutter, crumbs and stains,
A dark new tyrant took his seat and watched
The smoking wick, the final fall of wax,
From the last night when Love was lord.

HE SWEARS

'No more actresses,' this is what he swears,
This wealthy older man with a weak spot for
A pretty face, a modulated voice,
A flair for imitation.
'No more actresses,' he swears, with their
Always wanting a new part, always anxious
To hasten off to the next show,
Always falling in love forever
For six months, with the latest leading man,
Always wanting to make a scene,
Always wanting to slam doors,
Always alert to the main chance,
Willing to wipe out the world for
A great line, a great exit, a scene involving tears.
'No more actresses,' he swears and looks at his watch.
He hurries away. There's a new show.
He's made the acquaintance of one of the players.
She's twenty-three; hope springs up in his heart.

SHE SWEARS

'No more leading men!' This is what she swears,
The actress past her prime, hurrying through the rain.
'No more thinking I'm really in love,
Caught up in my own pretence,
No more credence in false worlds,
Lines invented by others,
Noble words uttered by no ones,
No more narcissists tricking, tricked by themselves
As much as tricked by me.
How I long for a real life with a real man
In a real world,
Someone steady and kind, someone who
Knows the meaning of love,
Isn't just saying the words and
Getting his buttons undone.'
She adjusts her coat, the rain's getting in.
She hastens her step, it's first call soon.
She hastens her step, she'll see him soon,
They get on so well, there's a real spark,
There's a definite bond, you can tell.

ANGEL

I spent five months by lakes and streams
Collecting pinions and primaries, feathers
Of purest white. Some were from geese
But most, I think, from swans.

All these I took to my house, and then
With scissors and thread, with sorcery,
With utmost craft, with supple wood,
I made them into wings.

You put them on, you loved their heft,
You stretched them out and ran.
You flew as if true born for flight
And as you flew, you sang.

I watched you changing, lovely, sublime,
Becoming the angel I'd guessed in you,
Until one day I came upstairs
And all I had left was a hair on the pillow
Of purest gold and a crease in the bed
And a long white feather
You'd shed by the window
And the golden ring I'd gone downstairs to fetch.

THE CURSE OF WINGS

And yesterday, in the afternoon,
An angel came to the bedroom sill,
And offered me her pristine flesh
For just one humid summer night.

She offered up six hours of bliss,
Unique and strange and mystical,
Weird and feral, timeless, wild, a world
Of incandescent heat and light.

I begged her stay. She swore that this
Was all her questing soul desired,
Her sweetest, cherished, yearned-for wish;
But such as she were left no choice.

She took my head between her hands
And kissed my mouth and pledged her heart,
Her voice and eyes were dark with grief;
She said that God lays down these things.

Then dawn inflamed the eastern sky
And suddenly she rose and sped
From bed to window ledge, to open sky,
And left me ruined by the curse of wings.

MISTAKES

I looked behind and saw the long straight line of my
    mistakes,
Faithful as hounds, their eyes alert, trailing in my wake.
    But
They weren't dogs, they were women, some fair, some
    dark,
Most of them young, all in tawdry, poor disguise,
In loose seductive gowns, faces concealed behind veils. But
I wasn't deceived; I knew them well, their swaying hips,
The wide glow of their innocent eyes.

I turned and spoke; 'Fair maids, why follow? You who
Helped me destroy all that was good, all that promised
    well?
You who dragged me always up wrong forks,
Bade me climb mountains of sheer unscalable rock in place
Of the gentle hill, who gave me specious reasons for
Turning gold to dung, silver to tinplate, instructed me
In alchemy, initiate and adept in the Temple of Disgrace.'

The chief Mistake, the fairest by far, said 'Master,
We follow you, we your disciples, your faithful friends,
Apostles, evangels, we guard and steer you on the uphill
    road, and
If not for us, what would you be? In storm and rain

Cyclone and wind, we are your milestones, we the ones
    you truly love,
We are the makers of memory, the deepest pangs in your
    heart,
Always with you, present and eager for when you need us
    again.

HIPPODAMIA, DAUGHTER OF BRISEUS

And now that I am old, the last that's left of Troy,
Fit for naught but stirring pots and watching babes,
I have at last the peace to wonder what it meant,
This life I led as traded thing, from man to man,
From land to land, fair-cheeked, fair-formed,
Most sweet of mind, most pretty prize of war,
Evil succeeding evil always through my days.

When young, they gave me to Minas.
He took me unbroken and broke me,
The first good man to warm my heart
In Afrodite's bed.
If love has a thousand faces,
With one of those faces I loved him.

Then he of the shining helm, the swift of foot,
Short-lived Achilles, sliced him down with the honed blade;
His armour clattered about him,
The dark mist clouded his eyes.
My city was burned, my people torn
With sharp, bright, terrible, hateful bronze.
He slew my brothers, took me slave,
He kept me bound in his dark-hulled ship.
In the curved walls he shut me in.
And then amongst the Myrmidons,

With music at my ears and flowers in my hair,
In grain-giving Phthia he wed me.

He called me sweet, he said I intrigued him.
He told me not to reproach him,
For such are the prizes of battle,
For this is the flow and ebb of sorrowful war.
He swore by grey-eyed Athene
To love and protect me as long as he lived,
Aware, as he was, of his imminent end.

With him I travelled the fish-swarmed, wine-blue sea,
Refused the lecherous, jealous hands
Of Atreus' godlike king. I refused his gifts,
His promise I spurned, I scoffed at his threats,
And once I held a sharp bronze blade to my tender throat,
    said
'Send me back to Achilles! Touch me once, and I die!'

Strange how love might grow on rocks,
Creeping from cracks like the blue flower.
Though slayer of Minas, Achilles was lovely,
Swift of foot, honour-hungry, most beautiful and doomed.
If love has a thousand faces,
With one of those faces I loved him.

Burdened with years, bent in the back,
In exile, so far from Lyrnessos,
Nothing now but the grave of those I loved in

Tawny youth, in the honeyfed days of innocent dance.
And now I'm fit for naught but stirring pots
And the watching of babes,
I who was fair-cheeked Briseis,
Once most comely of side-glancing girls,
Whose bed was never her own.

But when I drift, sweet bondmaid of sleep,
When with the back of his hand Morpheus brushes my
    eyes,
Patroklus comes to my couch
In sorrowful, backyearning, wistful dreams;
Not as he was when Hektor hacked him,
When he was felled and his armour clattered about him,
When down I plunged to my knees, his corpse in my arms,
Tearing my breasts and my hair, lamenting;
But as he was when he told me, lifting me clear
From the body of Minas, back in smoking Lyrnessos,
'Briseis, fairest of side-glancing girls, you must not weep;
For this is the flow of the tide of war.
Loathsome Ares grieves and wounds us all.
None but the gods know why the gods are cruel.
Come, you must go with your new lord,
He who was held by the heel, Achilles.'

If love has a thousand faces,
With the loveliest face I loved him, Lord of the people,
Most kind, most good, most courteous,
Most faithful of faithful friends;

Flowing of hair, more godlike than wide-browed Zeus;
He that I would have loved if Kytherea's will
Had blown my flesh where the heart lists,
Most gentle, most yearned-for Patroklus.

And when the dark mist clouds my eyes,
Although he never knew my bed,
I'll seek him first in Tartarus.

THE MAN WHO FELL IN
LOVE WITH THE MOON

He'd drunk too much, went out for air,
Felt the gravel beneath his feet,
Breathed in the pines, hearkened to owls.
There were no clouds. He sought the Plough,
The North Star, Venus shining, Mars rising.
All was shadow and silver, cold and pure.
There was little meaning to time.
Inside, his friends told jokes,
Drank wine, ate rice, and laughed.
He walked away, looked up.
It was hanging above the house,
Brilliant, pocked with lakes and seas,
Calm, benevolent, majestic,
Female in heart and womb.
With hands in his pockets
He gazed and gazed. He was
Mesmerised. He stood for an hour,
Tracked it across the skies,
Walked it around the horizon,
Forgot his friends, ate what grew by the road,
Grew cold as steel, thin as a blade,
Lived alone forever,
Unfit for human love.

FOR SYLVIE, WHO BELIEVED IN REINCARNATION

The news from France arrived last month
That you were dead and cloaked in earth,
The same dark earth your mother wears,
Who lies beside you silently.

We loved when we were young, not well,
But well enough and questingly.
We roamed about the southern hills
And lay in wheat till darkness fell.

You loved the ducks in English parks,
The ancient crones with bags of bread.
You paunched the lure of wild ideas
And let them fizz inside your head.

Your son arrived from France last night
To look for you in those you loved.
He has your eyes and could have been
My own, if I'd not taken fright.

So I've outlived and you've gone on,
Your body cold and cloaked in earth,
Deep-planted in the soil of France,
To wait, perhaps, your second birth.

THIS BEACH

The night grows tired; it shrinks and coils from eager
    fingers' reach.
The teeming days drag down in undertow
The timeworn pebbles of this sorry beach.
And we have worn like them; we hearken back
To the jagged edges of unmouldedness,
When the spirits rose and the sense adored
This hurtling and this dragging of the waves.

Our little corners of experience we cover with tarpaulins;
We do not seek the consolatory, tenderly listening friend,
Nor seek the tepid medicine of a repetitious bliss.
We wait like patient statues, wondering how it happens,
What it will be like, this promise unfulfilled,
This wakening with a kiss.

HE THINKS SHE THINKS

Because he wears bifocals, she thinks he must be clever.
Because his backside's tidy, she thinks he must be sensual.
Because his eyes are grey, she thinks he must be honest.
Because he's that much older, she thinks he's more
 dependable.

Because she has resplendent breasts, he thinks she must be
 clever.
Because her mouth and nose are small, he thinks she must
 be sweet.
Because her eyes are brown, he thinks she must be honest.
Because she's young and new to love he thinks she wouldn't
 cheat.

RAVEN

So let's not talk of how it was; that it was this
Or it was that; that we were innocent as doves.

Our joy was this: a raven that grew slow and fat,
Well-gorged on eye and heart and gut of older loves.

AH, FRANCESCO

Ah, Francesco, please! Enough of tears
And eyes like stars or suns or dawns that deign
To glance your way from time to time; and
Chaste heart and chaste hands that left a glove in yours
And caused your foolish heart to thrill with joy.

Enough of puns on laurel trees, enough
Of gentle *l'aura*, who, of course, is like
A summer's breeze, and, O Francesco, please,
Cease this weeping, stop this sighing, make
An end of faking her as painted saint.

If sighing, wailing, fainting's all you do,
Of course she's disinclined to sleep with you.

TUS OJOS DE SELVA

En tus ojos de la selva
Caimanes y capybaras son,
Ciervitos, y tapires, y picaflores.
En tus ojos de la selva
Orquideas y enredaderas son,
Ocelotes, tigres, pirarucus son.
Hay también, querida,
Un corazón desconocido
Por mariposas adornado.
Detrás de tus ojos morenos de la selva
Vivire, sin vacilar, sin esperanza,
Sin nunca regresar con luz o con vida.

OSIRIS PRAISES HIS WIFE

My wife, sister of Nepthys, mother of Horus,
Your eyes are dark with conquered grief, the dew
Of your thighs is sweeter than rain in greener
Places than this. Your flesh is perfect like silk,
Your breasts drip honey, your tresses are darker
Than dead stars that throw no heat or light.
If you demand it, hills bow down, the moon
Drops pearls on grass. When once you found the tree
In which I was entombed, you followed me
Beyond the further side of life, restored my breath;
You worked with clay, you made my body whole.
I love you, since you raised me up from death
And made me new, enthroned me by your side,
With gratitude and tenderness and pride.

I TRAVELLED MILES

I travelled miles to reach that place,
With heart and mind oppressed.
I cursed the wasted time,
The fallen slice of life,
The further pointless quest.

But there you stood, Greek maid,
With fair white skin, brown eyes,
A knowing smile, dark hair,
Black dress, black shoes, soft lips
Well-forged for love and lies.

Despite my present peace,
When hopes are small and few,
I'll mourn my greedy youth
And envy any other man
Whose hungry gaze alights on you.

DOVES

I saw a dove upon my roof,
Who shuffled shyly near his love.
He ruffed his neck and shook his beak
And warbled words of tenderness.

She listened to the words he said,
He leaned to preen her pretty head.
But ploys of love too well she knew
And did what pretty doves must do.

She shook her wings and off she flew.
He followed her and craned his neck
And sidled up and tried anew.
I laughed and thought of me and you.

AFTER PETRARCH

Exactly there at the left-hand window seat,
She glanced and looked away, and glanced again.
By the front door she sang a snatch from a song,
But then the words escaped her and she frowned.
Just here she caught my arm and pointed out
A child that leapt and cartwheeled on the lawn.
Beneath this tree she told me of her plans.

Under the archway, sheltering from the rain,
She said a thing that wounded, saw me wince
And look away, and sadly touched my cheek.
At the table there, she took a berry, put
It in my mouth, and laughed and stroked her hair.
Beyond the bridge, when out for air, she saw me,
Waved and called and hastened up to meet me.

At this oak door she turned, her hand upon the latch.
Out on the terrace, she scorned and mocked me.
Beyond those trees, in a field of wheat, and then
Amid the willowherb, she stamped and crushed
A place to lay a tartan rug, held out
Her arms to draw me down. The rooks and swifts
Ignored us, from their vibrant patch of sky.

One naked dawn she rose, to let her feet
Know chill new dew, then back she came to bed.

From the shoe-mender's modest shop she bought a pen,
A star-signed leather fob, an extra key.
Upstairs she wrapped them well in crimson foil,
Bound them about with ribbon, wrote a card,
And here, in this hallway, offered them to me.

LETTER TO AFRODITE

My Lady Afrodite, pleasant smiling girl,
If ever I have pleased you,
If ever I have done your will,
If ever I have made you laugh,
Then hear my prayer.

Lead me no longer, lady,
Where thorns disgrace the rose.
Mock me no longer, lady,
Do not abandon me, leave me to gag
In cesspits of despair.

Lady of the flowing hair,
If you would have me praise your name,
Then let me not devour myself,
Annealed to hellish misery
By hideous heat of self-fired flame.

And bring me one I sometimes faintly see
As if she were a memory.

TERMINUS

Between the schism of East and West
He juggles with the hammer and the dollar.
Between the chasm of soul and matter,
She struggles with the spirit and the thing.

Summer seasons flake away the surface
And the lineament and time reveals
The sculpture beneath the sculpture,
The sculptor beneath the sculptor,
The threnody that drones beneath
The long-exhausted, clapped out bacchanal.

His is an old mind in young man's clothes;
The old mind sharp, but ripe for resignation;
His body sharp and sweet for assignation.

He'll meet the woman's train, and down
At the river's edge, with the dace leaping,
Ignored by grazing waterfowl and cows,
She'll lean against a willow tree, avert
Her eyes and cancel out their vows.

THE NYMPH OF THE POOL
JUSTIFIES WHAT SHE DID TO
HYLAS

Don't look at me like that, and what's it got to do with
    you?
His mouth was soft and red, his beard was hardly grown
    and not
Yet trimmed. And how could I resist him, when I came up
    from
The depths? I paused, amazed, then threw my arms about
    his neck.
He cried out once, I drew him down, I kissed his virgin
    lips.
I did not let him drown. I brought him up, I bore him to
The bank. I sealed his eyes, his mouth, and called my sisters
    round.

They stood and laughed and said they envied me my lovely
    prize,
And stripped his shining armour off, and rubbed his limbs
    with oil.
He gazed at us in wonder, unbelieving of the joy.
They led him, ox-like, to the cave behind the bubbling
    spring,
And laid him on a bed of leaves and waited at the door,
To keep him in, until I had prepared myself for love,
And laid beside him softly, with my cool hand on his thigh.

It's true, I took him from his friends, his ship, his Herakles.
I first obeyed my eyes, that locked with his when up I came,
And then obeyed my heart, and then obeyed the voice
    below,
The voice that shouts or whispers from the loins,
    commanding me
With toothless mouth, that has its hungers, greeds and salty
    thirst,
Its own fine fleece (more lovely far than that which Jason
    sought),
And tells me what is pleasant-smiling Afrodite's will.

It's all her fault. I'm not to blame. And even if I were,
What's that to you? I'm no Athene, nor some Sinope,
Who scorns a lusty man or God and wallows in virginity.
It's not as if I did him wrong; I bind his brow with leaves
Of oak, he drinks my body's nectar, I spoon divine ambrosia,
I have his own bronze jug that he let fall, and out of that
I pour him wine that fills his flesh with heat and love and
    pleasure.

He'll not go back to Herakles, that roaring, lionclad brute,
Who's always mad with rage and whirls his club and leaves
    a trail
Of rape and wreck and broken skulls. I'd never yield him
    back –
He'd never choose to go – just look at lovely Hylas now,
My husband, my captive, my maker of wonders that flare
    and dance in my

Ever-youthful flesh. He'd never return to Herakles; he's far
    too drunk
With bliss, eager for my breasts, my hands, my belly, my
    embraces.

I loose my gown, release my nightdark hair, unleash my
    limbs;
I wrap my slender legs about his golden thighs and hips.
I spared this boy the common lot of feeble, mortal man,
And where I walk or swim, his heart flies after me; I hear
It flutter in my wake as if it flew to seek its nest.
We've made our vows, as pleasant-smiling Afrodite knows,
He'll serve my greed and need, as I'll serve his, at her
    behest.

These are my nymphs, this is my pool, my bed
Of leaves, where neither blood nor tears nor time
Have leave to flow. I rule this perfect place,
So wander on, and take your Book of Rules,
And take your disapproval when you go.

NOTE: Sinope was a girl who had resolved to remain a virgin, and
she tricked both Zeus and Apollo into letting her remain so.
Athene was likewise committed to virginity. Hylas was the beloved
servant of Herakles, who had killed Hylas' father in battle.
Herakles and Hylas set off with the Argonauts, but Hylas was
abducted by the nymph of a pool, and Herakles was accidentally
left behind by the Argonauts whilst looking for him.

LETTER TO PAULA

I dreamed of you again last night.
We did some very ordinary things.
We went to see your mother, went
And walked in the woods.
You wore your tight black jeans,
Your blue grey coat, your silver cross.
We held hands and were happy;
It must have been, I think, our early days.
Your mouth was small, your eyes
Enormous, deep enough to dwell in.

We made love, fell asleep.
I dreamed I was older, writing
Of us when young.

I haven't seen you, heard a word,
For more than thirty years, but
I thought I would tell you
That you were my body's finest hour;
That you survive in wishful, wistful
Filmy worlds of dreams,
Queen of longing, Empress of flame,
Knave of hearts, evasive companion,
Subtle liar, futile passion.

THE WOMAN TAKEN IN ADULTERY

When I returned to my husband's house intact,
Untouched by spiteful stones, incredulous,
I stood outside that hated door and knew I'd not go in.
I knew he'd strike me, take a blade to my throat,
That jealous man who loved me and loathed me,
Knuckled my face, demanded death for my sin.

I turned and went, retraced my steps, intact,
And sought out Mary's son. And there he was,
In the same place, weighing a rock in his hand.
He'd waited, knowing I had to leave, abandon all,
Travel away with him. I served him well. I quelled
His doubt. I gave him courage, broke with grief at the end.

I AM JEALOUS

After Sappho

This woman – who kneels before you where you sit,
And hangs on every word you say; admires your rings
And bangles, asks you how you curled your hair –
I think she's like a goddess – Artemis at least –
Who, hunting on Parnassus, heard your heart,
Flung down her bow and sped here from above.

You stroke her cheek and laugh. My outraged hopes
Rebel. My voice won't come, my tongue's dried up.
Sad disappointment snuffs my fading flame,
Your sparkling laughter mocks my foolproof schemes.
I'd never guessed what she's discerned – that you
Were forged to forage for the other kind of love.

A SHORT NIGHT

After Sappho

I do remember that night that fled so fast,
When we were golden, beautiful and young,
When dawn surprised us from her yellow throne
And filled the room with gathering song.

Your face shone back at me, your lovely hair
Spread out across your breasts, your hand caressed
My face. You said, 'Let's always remember this.'
I said, 'I wish these nights were twice as long.'

I GO TO THE BEACH

Why must I go to the beach
And search among the weed,
The faded lumps of wood,
The ropes and broken shells?
The hoopoe came and brought
A note from Sheba's queen
To warn me of your lips.
From the cypress, the bulbul
Sang in spring a sad song to the new rose;
Why do you bloom so sweetly
For one month only?
I crossed from the churches and mosques
To the houses of ruin,
But no one would take my worn-out cloak
In payment for wine.
He who preaches abstinence
Is at war with God.
My love, when you come to bed,
Bring your hands, your smooth arms
And perfumed hair.
Love me with fabulous excess
Till the red wine of the sun's light
Is poured out from the flagon of the East.
The wine of the grape,
The wine of your love
And the wine of dawn

Are like the breath of Jesus.
You pierce my soul with arrows;
I cannot survive the archery of your eyes.
Leave your clothes where you cannot find them;
Leave your shoes at the door.
Bring wine, for, all my life,
Love has been the enemy of my peace.
These decades of amorous tears
Have washed my brains to the sea.
I go to the beach and search,
In case they've washed ashore.

BY THE TIME YOU GET TO THE GATE

Outside the lightest of rains damps down the dust.
A lustful robin sings from his throne of thorn.
It's early, but share just one more meal with me;
By the time you get to the gate, all that we shared will be
    gone.

IF I HAD KNOWN

After Rumi

If I had known how cruel love is,
How savage, pitiless and dire,
I'd not have entered in his house,
But stayed outside to beat a drum
And warn the eager crowds away.
But now I'm here, inside the house,
I'm drumless, helpless, beaten, dumb.

THE TOMB OF LAOTHOE

Laothoe raised this tomb
To house the bones of one she found
Stretched out upon the beach
In foreign clothes a fortnight dead
But wondrous in the loveliness
That strangely lingered on;
And this she did with firm intent
In token of what might have been
That this will also be the tomb
That hides her bones when she has gone.

THE SPEAR

This spear that thumped into the ground
Between us both –
I'll feed it with dung,
Make it take root, grow leaves,
Blossom, become a shapely tree,
Bring forth fruit;
And so confound what you intend
By dragging evil through my door,
By setting traps
And hurling stones and spears at me.

AFRODITE'S REPLY

After Sappho

My dear man, I never did desert you.
Not like that hussy, who scuttled away
And took your purse and turned up later on
In the bed of an amateur actor, paralysed with wine.

It's me who should reproach you for your lack
Of faith. I could have come at any time.
I love you just the same in Cyprus,
In Cythera or Ithaka or Thebes.

And don't blame me if the hussy scuttled off.
It wasn't me who chose her, it was you.
If once you'd thought to ask me my advice
I would have told you 'Not at any price!'

My baffling light and heat outdo the sun –
I'm shining on you now, morose, complaining one.
I found a lovely girl not far away
And made her eyes snag yours just yesterday.

IT IS TIME

It is time to ease your burden down
And venture to the fastness of these strong but empty arms.
Let us discard regret
And all our lurking memories;
Let us now forswear
Our grimy histories.
Let us sleep entwined
And consider each other's dreams;
Let us awake to life and warm our hands,
And let our suns give light
And glow upon this wilderness.
Let us laugh, run like children
Bred to brighter lands;
Let us kiss on cold nights,
Forgetting we are old.
Let us jeer at death
And, falling fair at last of life,
Be strong,
Be sweet,
Be bold.

THIS LOCK OF HAIR

This lock of hair at the back of the drawer,
How long has it been there?
Twenty, thirty, forty years?
It's tied in a band of delicate lace.
Its colour is auburn, almost red.
It has no lingering scent.
How lovely she must have been,
This misremembered girl.
I test it between my fingers,
Perhaps my cheek remembers, my lips.
Ah, now I know whose it was,
This auburn relic I found at the back of a drawer.

LINES WRITTEN IN BATH, NOVEMBER 2013

He was small and young, a little mad no doubt,
Reciting Milton in the Abbey's shade
To the honeyed stones, to those who passed
That engine of light, with its delicate ceilings, walls
Overcrowded with tributes, epitaphs,
Portraits of conjugal, filial love,
Love to the grave and beyond.

He was dressed in doublet, cloak and hose,
Wore buckled shoes, a jaunty cap.
He caught our eye, was newly believing,
Drunk on the power, the love of Christ,
The promise of life hereafter, sweet redemption.
By heart he'd learned his Milton, all for the love,
The glory, the pleasure of God.

He caught us. We listened, trapped by pentameter,
The fabulous verse, the spark of his eye;
'Of man's first Disobedience, and the Fruit
Of that Forbidden Tree, whose mortal taste
Brought death into the World, and all our woe,
With loss of Eden . . . '

We'd gone in my antique car, broke down,
Then found at length our cheap hotel,

With its stuffy rooms and its nylon sheets.
We found a bistro, under the street,
A tarted-up basement, just perfect for us.
I gave you a snail, your very first snail,
Draped in parsley, drowned in garlic and butter.
It must have been Pierrepont Street,
North Parade, somewhere near to the river.

It was early days; you were all agog
With new delight. You were doing your best.
I felt like a victor, home from the wars.
You were working hard, you hadn't seen off
Your rivals, it was utterly clear that you would.
I knew already; it was you and no other;
To hell with them all, to hell with the rest.
You, the home of my soul; mine, the home of yours.

We were caught by adventure, responding
To Love's unreasoning, reckless, insidious call.
Though you were young, I was not too old;
All was pristine, clean as dawn,
Your hand in mine, mine in yours, as
Outside the Abbey, the Christian boy in his
Tudor clothes recited the tale of the Fall.

How far since then we have fallen away
From our dreams. You gave them up,
Your Glory Days; you lost your compass,
Cast yourself out of the circle, settled for dross,

Pulled us over the brink. You dropped
The baton, doused the torch, fell
Asleep on the job, fell
Further than me, it seems. And I'm
All fury like a shackled beast, like
Milton's devils, fallen angels,
Sitting brooding, bitter, by a vast abyss.

The Christian boy has travelled on.
There's no one speaking Milton
In the Abbey's shade, to the honeyed stones,
To the passers-by. And we have come to this;
There'll be no stone in any nave;
I will have from you no epitaph,
No conjugal tablet etched with faith,
No promise of love undying, reaching past the grave.

You and I were prelapsarian once,
In the Abbey's shade, in a town of honeyed stone,
Where a Christian boy was punch drunk,
Smitten by God and redemption, reciting Milton.

How far I have fallen with loss of Eden:
Ten years I travelled, from joy to disbelief.
How far you have fallen:
Ten years you travelled, from Huntress
To Lover, to Millstone, to Liar, to Thief.

AND NOW HE'S GONE

And now he's gone, she thinks how generous he was,
That possibly his patience failed from being tried too far,
Was battered, wrenched, eroded to the bone.

And now he's gone, she understands he loved
Her with a steady mind, was not a bird of passage
As her many other, slyly smiling loves.

And now he's gone, she counts them back,
The slow and blighted years she wasted in his wake,
When nothing came of what she hoped would come.

This scene was foreordained. My friends,
She staged a wondrous drama, weeping by his bed,
And finds she loves him truly now he's dead.

SKELETON SERVICE

'I have the account with the monthly amount
And the requisite number of kids, and so
I'm sorry to have to announce,' she said,
'Reductions in services, now to be subject to cuts.

No more rugs in the wheat field, my love.
No more languorous, horizontal hours.
No more sentimental deeds and,
Above all, nothing one might call French.

You will mow the lawn and clip the trees
And kindly keep out of the light, my love.
Do the odd jobs, remember my birthday,
And (of course) our anniversary.

Keep the money flowing, empty
The bins, stop your whingeing and wanting,
Stop complaining, sit where you're told
And keep the tiller steady.'

He nods his head and leaves the house,
His vengeance planned,
His consolation ready.

I AM AT WAR WITH TIME,
THE VILLAIN

I am at war with Time, whose villainy is to take
The perfect thing he wrought and then resculpt it.
Time's the eternal amateur, who cannot leave
Alone that first-flush inspiration, but
Takes a clumsy chisel, knows not where to stop,
And chips and changes, weakens and destroys it.

When I was new, unmarred myself by Time,
Longing for her through nights that seemed unending,
Half-awake, hot in bright blood and dreaming,
I thought I knew her modest, new-grown breasts,
The slender thighs, the golden plateau of
That soft, flat, adolescent belly.

I thought I felt that heavy fall of hair
And heard that low, calm, Desdemona voice.
I lost her soon enough, but people tell me
(Those who travel from the forest where she lives)
That eyes and voice remain, the eyes and voice I loved.
They say she thought me handsome in my day.

I am at war with Time, the villain that destroyed
And gave, shaped and wrecked, hacked away our beauty,
That Sacrilegious Beast, who gnaws his own sweet child.
I've warned him, should he take those eyes and voice,

Those best among the lovely gifts he gave,
I'll do my duty, deeds impossible and wild.

I'll take a blade. I'll hone it on the wheel of hate.
I'll track him down. I'll rip his entrails out.
I'll flay his skin and hang it from the trees.
I'll throw his liver to a nest of rats.
I'll break his yellow teeth. And cut his throat and
Kill him.

ON ARTHUR'S SEAT

Let us
beware of falling rocks
And walk the upward of the weary track,
And let us unkey the rustbound locks
And tell the wind we'll not turn back
From all this foolish, shamestained love
That drives us on, yet stands and mocks.
Let us now determine
Our rare, exquisite opportunities.
If those who love like us are birds of prey,
Buzzard, owl and hawk, and kite and merlin, let's stoop
Like them, when chance affords,
And plummet from above.
Wrenched on by rage, desire and spite,
We two selfish raptors, who seize
The day, but rip the dove, perch on
This windwrecked, rainwhipped height,
And watch the norsebound ships go sailing,
Catching from meadows, worlds below,
The flowering, sorrowing, fate-foretelling
Notes of a lone piper
Wailing.

ROMANCE IN A BARGAIN BOOKSHOP

He leans against the bookcase, casually, it seems.
He loves her shop but partly for the books
And partly for the mischief in her manner.
He knows that she is older by a generous twenty years,
Her children gone, her firm flesh flown
Bit by bit by fraction, and always and as usual
It's crueller far for woman;
He grows surer, she grows sad;
He numbers what he has; she numbers what she had.
It's crueller far for her, but even so
He feels no pity when he leans against the bookcase,
Casually, it seems.
He'd stay all night, without compassion, so would she,
For pleasure in the nuanced conversation.
He leans against the shelves, this younger man,
She leans against the till, this older woman,
Entirely for the thrust and cut, the take and give,
The play of this flirtation.

LAST AUTUMN

Last summer I conceived a plan, and so it was
I wrote to you on every leaf of every tree
In all the many gardens and the courtyards where you walk.
'Such wealth of leaves!' I said.
'She'll surely find my words.
She'll surely be impressed.
My words will captivate her heart.
She'll surely leave off others,
Surely love me best.'
The sun fell pale, the sky grew hard,
The autumn storms stripped off the trees,
And all the leaves swam down,
Swirled and spiralled, pranced their foolish dance,
Gathered on your paths,
Submerged your courts and lawns.
You swept them up and heaped them up
And stood and watched the smoke
As all of them you burned.
The ash you spread, enriching all your lands,
Erasing all my months of words
That never reached your heart
But only warmed your hands.

A WARNING

Her longing's like the sea,
Tempestuous, savage, sister to
The angry cat that springs to scratch the stars
And scrape the eyes of heaven.

Her longing's like the sea,
Sometimes serene,
Creator of the smoothly sanded shell,
Safe to sail on, sweet to swim in,
Warm and weedless, maidenbed of peace,
Good servant of your sleep.

Whatever, however it is,
Her longing's like the sea;
It chisels at your shores, it rips
Away your dunes,
And undermines your walls.

And then there comes the time,
With hands and limbs and eyes and lips,
She breaks your lighthouse,
Wrecks your harbours, salts the meadows,
Overspreads the good dark land
And drowns you in your ships.

YOUR GRACEFUL PATH

I went alone
And gathered pebbles from the same beach,
The exact spot where you came three times
Above my mischievous hand.
Will such illicit joy and such pretence of pain
Ever cross your graceful path again?

I went alone
And ordered tea at the same table
In Alexandra's café, out on the esplanade,
And laughed about what happened in the Ladies.
Will such outrageous joy and such pretence of pain
Ever cross your graceful path again?

I've made love since
With the wrong girl, with darkened heart, on the same bed
Where we gave birth to too much delectation.
Will such unfettered joy, such augury of pain,
Ever cross my straitened path again?

ON THE HACIENDA BALCONY

Come down, and lean your elbow there,
Your chin upon your hand.
Look out across that field and ponder.
The grass is high, not so?
Is not the rainy season driftwood
Still scattered on the ground?
And look, my friend, there winds the track
From that corral to stony fields beyond.
Bethink you of the times that you and she
Have raised a pall of dust
And galloped down that track,
Rejoicing in the valour of your youth,
Sombreros flying, hair caught up in wind,
Her white teeth flashing in her laughter,
Her strong thighs, her body, in such mastery of
The beast that pounds beneath her.
And here at last she comes, and here's
The storm of dust, and here she is.
She reins her horse and down she swings, this
Woman fit to be a tribe of heroes' mother,
Woman made of fortitude and will,
Woman bred of sunlight and savannah.

HIS STEADFAST EYES

And as that sword of yours
Sweeps down to slice his head
From his neck, though guiltless of harm,
He'll clench his hands to his sides,
Unflinching, and won't avert
His steadfast eyes from your face.

He trudged through the desert for this,
And waited outside with the poor.
He came here begging for nothing,
Not kindness, love or attention,
But just to witness your beauty,
His steadfast eyes on your face.

And when they stitch his lips
And block the holes of his corpse
And wrap him in rags, omit
The prayers and laugh as they shovel
The dirt, he'll still not take
His steadfast eyes from your face.

IT SEEMS TO ME

It seems to me this mighty lake
Has given birth to the moon, and
The moon hangs low, like a threat.

All day long I thought of you
And now I could cup my hands
And fill them with light
And keep it for you in a box.

I dowse the candle; it can't compete.
The dew has soaked my shirt, I shiver,
Return to the bed and my tawdry dreams,
Sorry that, after all, I had no light to save,
And cold, until our bodies meet.

PINPRICK

As the candlelight flickers on paint-peeled walls
And the cat sits lost in private ecstasy,
The clouds scud past, there is no moon or star,
And earth and sky are darkened, cold and smarting,
Stinging from the pinprick of an absence.

We who make merry after clash of arms,
Nonetheless keep corners of reflection,
Glean fluffballs of regret from underneath
Our nails and grow distract, nostalgic, silent,
Wounded by the pinprick of an absence.

YOU CAME TO SEE ME IN ST ANDREWS

You came to see me in St Andrews.
I met your coach, we wondered what to do.
I don't know what we did,
But walk the streets in rain.
It was too late, our ship had gone,
And there we were, stranded together,
Confounded sailors on a buckled wharf,
Our boat a speck in the distance,
Reduced to a feather of smoke.

And when you left on the same coach,
You mimed with one finger,
The wiping away of a tear from
The pale cheek that mine would never seek
To press again.

ARAB COUPLE INADVISEDLY HOLDING HANDS IN DUBAI

He in smart white cotton.
She, erased in black.
See merely the bridge of her nose,
The dark eyes sparking and laughing.
Forgetting themselves, they stroll by the palms,
Stop and look at the birds.
Their hands drift the distance,
Their fingers twine like vines.

For just one moment the dust of custom
Is wiped away by love.

BRIDGE, DON'T MOVE

After a Turkish folk song
recited to me by Zülfü Livaneli

Bridge, don't move, but stay where you are,

So that even should my best beloved

Not come, the hope may still remain.

ALL MY SALTY MEMORIES

And where did the dancing go,
The music and humid nights
We crammed with drunkenness and love?
I fear they were never there –
I might have made them up –
And all my salty memories
Are mere imagination.

It seems they tapered away,
But I do recall your soul and mine
Making those salty memories; and it
Wasn't a dream, but you and me
Breathing our lives to the same rhythm,
Beating time on the same tune,
Locked together in travel.

GYPSY GIRL

We sat and talked the morning through,
The girl and I, the Gypsy girl
Curled up in the red chair, with her
Chestnut hair tied back, her ringlets barely tamed,
Much like herself, no doubt. She drank my coffee,
Smoked her roll-up, munched on toast,
Told me of travelling, living right out on the edge,
Her rotten taste in men.

Her dark eyes shone, she laughed like water,
I could feel my heart in my chest,
Scared and alert, like the creature doomed
In the headlights's suns. I felt, for the first time in years,
The rancid taste of old worlds sweeten on my tongue,
The throb of new worlds pulsing in my throat.

And when she left, she embraced me
As if I were handsome,
As if I were kind, as if I were young.
And after she left, I sat in my chair and trembled.

But then the sun grew bitter, jealous, bade
The dark earth draw her down, and
She never came back, my Gypsy girl.

AND WHEN IN BITTER RAGE

And when in bitter rage you left this house
And made off with our life, and fled with
The first fool whose words were soft;
And when you laid this world to waste
And stabled nightmare in the naves and aisles
And smashed the windows' many-coloured glass;
And when you laid the axe to pews of worthy oak
And cut the pulls and broke the bells
That smashed with a clang of brass on stone slabs;
And when you trod your salt in beds of flowers;
And when you sought out thieves to steal our means,
Still you could not breach these keeps and towers.

For Love did not leave this castle,
But Love remained inside these massive walls.
Like woodbine, heavy with syrup,
Like bindweed, laden with bells of virginal snow,
Love grew and prospered in hall and room,
Love twined up banisters, seized
The legs of chairs, draped from lamps,
Half-hid the portraits, snared the incautious.
For when in bitter rage you left this house,
Love would not leave, Love held back at the door,
Love mocked your rage, remains with us,
And piles up wealth on table, stair and floor.

HER DISOBEDIENT FEET

And so she goes; she leaves her latest love,
And hopes that life might touch her
Gently with his finger.
No bitterness, no blame
And no recrimination. Just
The tailing of the song,
Abandoned by the singer.

She is very sorry, sorry indeed;
His love was so beguiling and so sweet.
Her heart remains, it's his,
But there they go! She follows them,
Her disobedient feet.

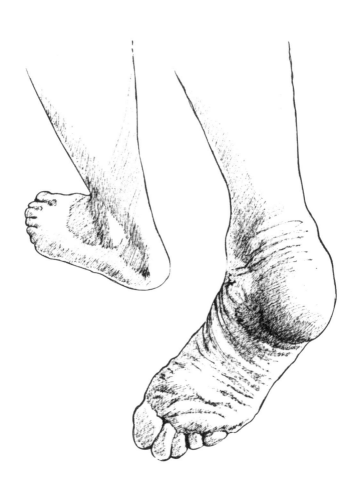

A TROPICAL PASSION (I)

He loves you because you are hotter than ají sauce,

He loves you because you search for fluff in your navel and
    then complain it makes your finger pong.

He loves you because you are more intoxicating than balché;
    your flesh is like a water-yielding vine.

He loves you because you bestride his back and knead him
    like bread when his muscles clench and knot.

He loves you because you complain of sweat in places riper
    than guava.

He loves you because, when angry, your black eyes flash
    like lightning on mountains, they glitter like stars
    reflected in water, and then your red skirts swirl as you
    turn and slam the door.

And later, bringing lemon and panela, you reach, and slide
    your hand inside his shirt, undo his buttons, say that you
    forgive him, take his hand, kneel down and pull him to
    the floor.

SONNET: I'LL MAKE NO HYMN

I'll make no hymn about your beauty, Lady; praise
Is undeserved where art and luck combine.
I'll make no pretty speeches, Lady, strike no
Noble poses, seek no clapped-out metaphors to mine.

I'll not discourse of sighs and tears and eyes that pierce
The soul. I'll not reprove you for your hardened heart
Or whine for pity, wheedle in by way of flattery,
When reciprocity was all I'd hoped for on your part.

I'll make no hymn about your sweetness, Lady; such
As yours defends you and conceals you. It's a wall.
There was a time I loved you captively, and now
I love you free. Times change. Tides turn. Boughs break.
   Towers fall.

I always thought you beautiful; still do, Lady.
I want you on my arm and in my bed, that's all.

ALREADY

The snow glows blue beneath a weight of sky,
The frozen moon is rimmed in borrowed light;
The old cat dreams, oblivious as the fire dies down.
An indifferent peace in the early hours,
And all the world too weary
Even for its necessary sorrows.

Her body smells of him.
Her falling eyes she'll not let sleep.
She'll watch the snow exhale
Beneath its carapace of frost.
Yet in this ship, this broad soft bed,
That's weighing anchor, leaving harbour,
How should she imagine storm or cold?

She already loves him, fearing his freedom,
His infinite resignation.
His wild and innocent ways corrupt her laws.
Already she must fear the thrust,
The blade between the breathing ribs,
When opening doors to strangers.
She wishes for another kind of world,
That's yet the same as this.

She'd wash him in streams and
Run with him in meadows.

She'd stud with hopes his heart's gold throne,
Like rubies set in ancient rings.
She'd freeze him now in free mid-leap,
And on his face he'd wear that strange,
Prophetic smile he always wears
At those odd moments when
He wishes that, and wonders if,
She might indeed, at last, be his life's love.

SHOULD YOU GO

Should you go,
The sun will blaze dark on summer days,
Raindarts fall of tempered steel;
Should you go,
Waves will roll back at spring tide
And wounds gape in earth's flesh
That cannot heal.

Should you go, birds will lay stones,
Cats bark and sheep stalk prey.
Stones will howl,
Gardens be dunes of dust of leaves,
And fish shoal in autumn wind.

Should you go,
Should love fall still,
Oaks will bud winter blossom
Of crimson jade, magenta snow
Rise up from levelled hill.

HE IS UNDETERRED

He is undeterred by your late-discarded
But malingering virginity,
Your hyperbolical fidelity.
He is undeterred
By the dark void, the deep abyss of your eyes,
The green sap in your bones,
Your deadly secret and its injury.

He is unconfounded by your dearth of years
And opposite opinions, your impudent
And imprudent, defiant décolletage,
Your small sharp teeth and catlike tongue.

He is unperplexed by your tropic, overheated room,
Your needless common sense,
Your prescient, pressing horror of the tomb.

He is undiscouraged when you flutter
Just not quite near enough the flame;
He loves your promise unfulfilled,
He loves your strange unruly heart,
Half-wild, half-tame.

YOU ENTERED IN MY HOUSE

After Sappho

Yesterday you entered in my house and
Took your violin and played 'Schön Rosmarin'.
The smile upon your face was like the light
Of one who suffers bliss beneath the body of her love.

This smile was my defeat.
God help my helpless hands.

Lavish your music on me, send your friends
Away. Subject me to your beauty and
We'll not walk to the wedding. Let me flame
As one who suffers bliss above the body of his love.

This music's my defeat.
God help my helpless hands.

THAT WILD CRY

When first I heard that wild cry
  It was the wind soughing
    In midnight's arms and shrieking.
      It was seagulls hurtling,
        Squabbling, screaming, mewing,
          It was unseen woodland creatures
            Wailing, keening, courting,
              The skies kicking, the leaves blowing.
                When first I heard that wild cry
                  It rose from throat and furrow
                    Of she who sped my sowing.

I WILL NOT SEE YOU

No, I will not see you.
It was in our youth,
You nearly left him for me.
Your body was small,
Your hair blonde,
Your eyes blue,
You did wonderful things with
Your tongue, your lips, your hands.

You had music you thought I would like.
It was how many nights?
Five at the most.
The other man won.

I have no wish to hear sad tales,
The terrible tales
Of all that happened next,
About your regrets,
About how your courage,
Your better nature, failed.

I want to see you forever,
Far in my mind's eye,
As you were when you brought me music
And shared my bed;
Five nights at the most,

When you gave me your
Beautiful, golden youth,
Untravestied by time.

THREE HAIKUS

I took her a pear.
She let it rot on a plate.
The tree's indignant.

———————

When I was twenty
I thought I'd try Spanish Fly.
It made no difference.

———————

When I was sixty
I thought I'd try Spanish Fly.
I didn't bother.

ON GIVING A SILVER HEART
TO A CRUEL LADY

Since you state that we must part
And no compassion moves your heart;
Since mine is useless, being dead,
Take this silver heart instead.

Your bed has not the space for me,
So let this lie where I should be,
Upon your breast, against your heart,
To lie there still, although we part.

THE LITTLE PARADISE

Not much more than a shed, two tiny rooms,
Obscured at the back of a yard,
Fronted by fields, shadowed by trees.

Here one day you were met by a hare,
That seemed to have something to tell you,
But thought it wiser to leave.

You thought you'd learn the mandolin.
A book was propped, you'd tuned the strings.
You pleased me, hoping to please.

A wooden chamber filled by a bed,
A languid lovers' room for idle afternoons
Made sacred by pleasures and sleep.

You'd lost your child, not mine, you said.
I came in haste, you took my clothes,
Began again on new life's quest.

We took wrong paths to the right place,
Our children by others grow apace,
And I still yearning for your voice and face.

AS THE CHILD

Just as the child on the North Sea beach
Will never tire of casting stones
That splash and grind in the green wave,
So do I persist with these,
My unregarded, tentative approaches.

Here is my hand; take it or not, it will wait a while,
Its fingers hopeful, ready to work,
To grasp the nettle, conjure joy,
To proffer mundane, ordinary gifts.

Just as the child on the North Sea beach
Will rummage for hagstones, feathers, shells
That lie amid the flotsam and the weed,
So do I seek what you would wish I'd give.

My body is ready; take it or not, this ruby
In my breast is not a meagre treasure;
Others have sought it, hoped to win it,
Prized it, used it with pleasure, wept at last for its loss.

Just as the child on the North Sea beach
Will shed her clothes when the sun breaks cloud,
So do I strip this armour from my soul
And brace my legs for the shock of waves.

I have come from my fortress; take me or not, I am patient
   and proud.
I do not kneel, do not bewail, do not beseech.
This is my heart, these are my hands. Take them or not,

I will sting in the sand whipped up by the wind,
Just as the child on the North Sea beach.

SYBILLE

Boughs break, leaves fall, life ebbs, our sun
Declines and chills, our beauty bleeds
Away, but here's the truth,
The strangely sweetened bitter pill:
Because you charmed my famished heart,
But also gently baulked my lust
And held me off, I love you still.

FOR TISHANI

The elegant bones, the smooth skin,
The black eyes, the pink gums,
The sharp white teeth, the dancer's hips,
The shining hair, the eloquent lips,
All the etceteras of a list like this,
May they never age nor fade.
But where's the hatch, the secret stair
That winds behind such eyes' delight?
This beauty is a barricade,
Such pristine surface scatters all the light.

MESSAGE TO RUMI

You once wrote down that on the day
You heard your first sweet tale of love,
You started looking, unaware
How blind and ignorant you were;
For lovers do not finally meet,
They're in each other from the start.

Old friend, I'd guess you were, the day
When first you heard that tale of love,
A little boy, as I was, unaware
Of how ephemeral you were.
And now I'm old and think I'll never reach
The one I loved within me from the start.

YOU HAVE RETURNED

After Sappho

At last you've returned and say you pined for me
As I have pined for you; saying that, even abroad,
You failed to be happy, the Cretan flowers made you sad.
You sent your thoughts to me, remembered my songs
In which I called you Holy, and, watching the night arrive,
Thought 'Now he prepares for bed and we can sleep
Together in dreams at the same time. And space
Will amount to nothing. And he will be my god again.'

The sun flares out, our lady the moon climbs up
And creeps across the cushion of the stars. She silvers
Down on the small waves of the salty sea
And down on the dewy fields and the gardens of roses,
The roadside lupins and mullein, and orchards
Where young girls wait for figs that slowly swell on trees;
Where I have passed so many hours in long dry grass
Waiting for you, pining, as you say you pined for me.

THE BED

What scandalous things it's seen,
This king-size bed in a small hotel!
Such tawdry scenes, affairs and one-night stands,
Infidelities, disasters, failures,
Bliss regretted, unattained, denied.
How bored this bed is with all that
Meaningless grunting and heaving,
The cords lashed to its bars,
The terrible mess, the weeping.

But now two gods have come
Disguised as no one at all:
Mr and Mrs Grey and Forgettable.

In darkness they peel their mortal skin
And the room glows gold.
A rich but subtle scent seeps
Into curtains, sheets, pillows and springs.
They are utterly lovely,
These gods who have shed their disguise.
Their skin is the colour of honey of thyme,
They are fashioned of amber light,
Hot as Aegean summer sand.
Who can they be, these exquisite souls,
Ancient and perfectly young,
Bound together in beautiful, tremulous joy?

Their eyes grow huge with desire.
Their laughter is light and unashamed.
The bed frame feels the shock,
The thrill, the electric force, the quivering pulse
Of the two gods, ancient and perfectly young,
Attuned to their pleasure
Like tautened strings of a lyre.

The gods have done; they
Dress again in their mortal skin –
Mr and Mrs Grey and Forgettable –
Pay their bill and travel on
To the next abode of bliss.

The bed settles back on its springs.
It has found at last its meaning,
The purpose of all that cutting, planing and joining.
'I was made,' it thinks 'for this.'

But the bed has become forlorn,
It has no further purpose in this room.
Its most magnificent hour has flicked away,
When two young deities stepped into Time,
Loved bright and long, loved without shame,
Mingled, laughed, caressed and kissed.

The bed waits. It will suffer the mortals.
It will wait and remember and yearn,
Against the day that might come to pass,

When the two gods, other gods, any gods
Return.

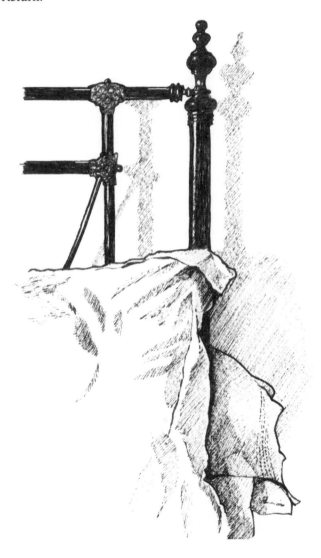

POEM ON THE BACK OF A SCRAP

Young woman, I see how lovely you are
With your black hair and your slick jeans
And your fake gold Gypsy jewels.

Young woman, your mother is with you
And I see how lovely she was, and my heart hurts
And I wonder what man it was who took her beauty
To make your beauty.

And I wonder what man it will be
Who will take your beauty,
So that one day, in a dark café,
A man like me will see your daughter
And write on the back of a scrap from a file
'Young woman, I see how lovely you are.'

ACHILLES MOURNS PENTHE-SILEIA

I braced my foot against her horse, and out I wrenched my
  spear of ash
With which I'd spitted both at once. She gasped and as she
  died I vaunted –
Jeered – said 'Woman, you should have stayed at home and
  done what other
Women do. What folly, vanity and pride made you come
  here,
So confident of triumph over me? What wine has made
  you drunk?
What god has ripped your wits away, daughter of Ares
  though you are?
Go lie in dust, be torn apart by dogs, let buzzards take your
  eyes and tongue.'

But when I plucked her helmet off, I stood appalled by
  what I'd done.
It was as if I'd lifted night from earth and raised the sun
  at dawn.
I dropped upon my knees and touched her deathstruck
  cheeks, her eyes and lips.
I saw no mortal beauty. In her armour there she lay, her
  mouth
In motion still, with unvoiced words, a prayer to Zeus to
  live at last.

She stroked me with the final glance of those most lovely
    eyes, and then
I knew, even in agony, exactly what this woman was.

My comrades gathered round and thought that she was
    Artemis asleep,
Exhausted from the hunt, or Afrodite, languid in her bed;
And each man thought his wife at home was dross and
    dust compared to this.
I cursed the gods, who sport with us like toys, then haul
    us down to shade.
And I was wild with penitence, and guilt; for she was beau-
    tiful,
Most tall, most strong, the one I might have loved. I held
    her head and wept.
I'd slain my longsought equal, who should have been my
    lifelove and my queen.

NOTE: With due acknowledgement to Quintus Smyrnaeus.
Penthesileia was a queen of the Amazons. She carved a trail of
corpses amongst the Achaeans, until she encountered Achilles.

FOR FEAR OF PARADISE

She wanted to kiss him, but he turned aside,
For fear of paradise.
She bared her body, but he could not look,
For fear of paradise.
She bade him dance, but he walked away,
For fear of paradise.
She bade him stay, but he left the land,
For fear of paradise.
My friends, believe me, he has travelled far
And taken risks, has sought his joys elsewhere,
For fear of paradise.

A TROPICAL PASSION (2)

He'd lie unclothed within the hammock of your limbs,
Would draw and drink the living sap and cram his mouth
With all your guava flesh, that fills his humid dreams,
That fevers up his loins and sets his throat on fire.
He'd strew a bed of leaves and shape it to your hips;
He'd watch for cayman in your swelling ponds and streams.

His face he'd bury in your tawny belly's shade,
And lay you on your back and taste your moistened lips.
He'd sting with ants and chase the blue macaws across
The trees, bent over in the cyclone of your sighs.
He'd disappear and not be found, without a map,
Without machete, in the jungle of your eyes.

THESE VERSES

'You may observe,' he said 'these verses
Copied out and set here on the wall.
An Alexandrian, renowned in Greece, wrote them
When he was young. Their message,
Though commonplace, is perfectly expressed.
You will agree, it has exquisite music,
Noble grandeur, pith and eloquence.

Here see Poseidon, here a mermaid, here a chest of riches,
Here a dolphin, here a ship in sail, and
See, a map of Ithaca, neatly underlaid.
Such calligraphic skill, such happy charm!
It's clear to all, she did it when her heart
Knew hope, was stirred and lit by love,
When she was innocent and young.

You may wonder that I keep it,
This gift from one who laid my peace
To waste, made off with those I loved.
Do not be so surprised; the poem stands
Sufficient in its lustrous self. And art is art,
No matter how the artist might betray.

And furthermore, it does remind me
Of my more successful, more delightful days;
And then, of course, as you no doubt will know,

They never leave, those twins, that stoic pair;
Though poor and withered, soiled and sour,
Tattered, ruined, twisted, torn,
Obscured by tawdry, reeking stains,
It always seems to come to pass, that
Something of Hope survives,
Something of Love remains.

HIS LOVE FOR YOU

He wears his love for you like prayer beads;
His humble salutations are a penance;
His wistful soul dissolves like salt, dispersing
To the four points of Earth's imagined corners,
Where he is drunk by fishes, exhaled into the skies,
Confected into rain, released on mountain peaks
To swell the streams, form crystals in the dark cold caves,
A dozen times and a dozen times again.

With old regrets he packs his trunks and cases,
Has paid out debts he had not planned to pay;
He ventures forth, is guided by
Our Lady of the Hopeless Expectations,
To whom we pray by night, but whom we mock by day.

By every nuance of your every limb,
By every flicker of your distant light,
By trudging where the spore of perfume leads,
By every futile gift, he reconfirms
That he is vapour, and all his love for you
He wears like prayer beads.

HOW ONCE, WHEN YOUNG

After Ronsard

When you are old and white and sewing by the fire,
Or reading verse by the lamp's soft light on winter days,
Some lines of mine may come to mind and you'll recall
How once, when young, you won a poet's love and praise.

Your long companion may be snoring by the fire
Or half asleep and staring at the flames that leap
And crackle in your grate. He may not hear or heed
If you should picture me or speak my name or weep.

And I'll be dull beneath the clay by then, shrouded
In shadow, wound in roots of trees, a boneless ghost,
While you waste by the fire, an old and faithful wife,
Who hearkens back to one who prized and pleased her
     most.

So let us live for now, my sweet reluctant love.
Relent and pluck today the roses of this life.

A TIME BEFORE SLEEP

There's time before sleep for grieving
That he is one day older, youth half-sped,
And she is not beside him there
While autumn winds above the beach
Whoop and wail to the crescent moon,
And trees weep leaves, their golden dead.

There's time before sleep for grieving
That one day soon he'll be drawn back
To journey to those smooth lithe limbs,
That warming flesh, and lie entwined;
That she has wound him in Arakne's thread,
Reluctant bondsman to her mad wild ways,
Her Celtic, lilting voice, her sudden moods
No sooner come than fled.

While autumn winds, carousing,
Whoop and wail to the crescent moon, dread
Becomes his mistress and companion,
Who toys with him and takes him to her bed.

PUT OUT THE LIGHT

Close the shutters,
Put out the light,
Place one candle on the shelf.
See, we are young again;
Our malformations, all life's
Etchings in our flesh are gone,
Are evened out, engoldened,
Softened by shadow.
Your hair smells sweet, your
Head in the crook of my arm, your
Hand on my chest.
We'll lie like this till the candle dies,
And then, in the dark, lie face to face.

They'll glitter like moonlight on water,
Our old, experienced eyes.

ANOTHER PRAYER TO AFRODITE

Pleasant-smiling, long-tressed Afrodite,
Who, turn by turn about, seduced, misled,
Surprised, bamboozled, pleased, abused, bemused,
Who threw me down and, laughing, raised me up,
Who teased, rewarded, robbed, beguiled, entangled me;
Accept this payment of my lifelong debt.

Make no more mischief, Lady, leave me be,
Vouchsafe me peace and calm and dignity,
Upon a distant day I hope may come,
When I might flare no more and then forget.
But do delay as long as you see fit
And don't come now. I'm not quite ready yet.

IN COLOMBIA

I opened my eyes and saw the sky.
I opened my ears and heard the racket
Of frogs and crickets and birds.
I savoured the vapour of rainsoaked grass,
And the hot sweet scent of horses.
And then, with my bare hands,
I parted my ribs, dug deep with my nails,
Wrenched my heart open, found some words.

Some were like gold, others like brass,
Bright in the palm of my hands,
Others like rubies and topaz.
In hope of deploying these beautiful words,
For lack of worthier treasure,
I stitched up my ribs, readied my tongue, prepared my
    arms.

In the house and terrace, and out by the stable,
I sought the one for whom these words were mined,
And found her at last, washing her horse in the river.

ACKNOWLEDGEMENTS

Due thanks to Brian Johnstone, who outed me as a poet at the St Andrews Poetry Festival and gave me the confidence to carry on; to Michael Hulse, who enlightens me on the subject of metrics, and is generous with advice and encouragement; to Donald Sammut, surgeon and artist, who is unafraid to be delighted; to Sofka Zinovieff and Victoria Hislop, warm-hearted readers of my first drafts; to Rachel Klausner for helping me edit on one of those frustrating newfangled computer things; and to my father Piers, who thought it a noble thing to be a poet, and would himself have made a life in poetry if the course of his career had not been diverted by Adolf Hitler.

'The Bed' first appeared in *The Warwick Review*. 'The Spear', 'All My Salty Memories', 'Angel' and 'Message to Rumi' first appeared in *Dream of a City* (Astrolabe Press, 2014).